50p

19

RENOIR

CHILDREN

PETITE ENCYCLOPÉDIE
DE L'ART

D0716306

© FERNAND HAZAN, PARIS 1958

DROITS DE REPRODUCTION RÉSERVÉS S P.A.D.E.M., PARIS

PRINTED IN FRANCE

RENOIR

CHILDREN

BY

RAYMOND COGNIAT

TUDOR PUBLISHING CO.

NEW-YORK

Renoir is the least intellectual of modern painters. Whereas the aim of other artists—to free themselves from social and aesthetic conventions—could not have been achieved without a whole series of theories, principles, and systems, Renoir's work, both in conception and execution, is entirely the reflection of his own temperament, and in fact no more than an expression of his tender and affectionate nature. His most voluptuous paintings always have an instinctive elegance which preserves them from vulgarity, without in any way diminishing their power of suggestion.

Compared with Renoir's, the pictures of the artists who may be considered his predecessors—Tintoretto, Rubens, Fragonard, Delacroix—natural though they are, look like the work of theorists, almost of intellectuals. The nature of Renoir's inspiration, and the very limited rôle of theory in his conception of painting are best illustrated by a well-known sally attributed to him : "I consider my nude finished when I feel like smacking her bottom." So much for dogma and brain-work ! But, of course, this does not mean that Renoir's work is devoid of thought or that it is inspired by mere vulgar materialism.

Refinement and affection are evident in all his pictures, but nowhere more clearly than in his numerous portraits of children. Many of these were commissioned during the period when, thanks to the friendship of Victor Charpentier and his family, he was a welcome visitor in intellectual middle-class circles, and his touching portraits of their children were the delight of many parents. The loving attention lavished on these pictures shows that the man, as well as the painter, was stirred by the sight of fresh faces and charming attitudes. It is clear from the portraits of Mme Charpentier and her children, the Mlles Cahen of Antwerp (pl. 15), and later the Caillebotte children (pl. 8) that though the choice of subject was imposed by the terms of the commission, it was also a source of personal satisfaction to the artist.

The existence of this sympathetic relation between subject and painter is already visible in Renoir's earliest pictures, particularly in the portrait of Mlle Lancaux, painted in 1864; but it is much more obvious in the portrait of *Mlle Legrand* (pl. 1) or the *Girl with a Watering-Can* of 1876 (pl. 2). Mothers, too, liked to have themselves painted with their children, visiting their friends, out walking (pl. 4), or in the privacy of their wealthy homes.

Unlike most portraits, Renoir's, though they bear the unmistakeable imprint of their time, particularly as regards fashion in clothes, are more than mere souvenirs, and of more than topical interest. In his own way, Renoir has made them into a series of allegories of maternal love and childish grace, a tendency particularly pronounced between 1880 and 1883. We are more conscious of the artist's feelings than of the social class of the sitter; the women may belong to the bourgeoisie but first and foremost they are mothers and their children are just charming babies, whom they suckle or embrace, in accordance with the gentle ritual of maternity. Elsewhere Renoir's drawing takes on a certain austerity as it becomes more precise, but it

GIRLS AT THE PIANO. 1882.

remains touchingly sensitive when he is dealing with children.

When Renoir paints a portrait, he is never merely doing a job and trying to please a customer; it is always a matter of personal interest to him, and indeed in some of the later pictures, painted when he himself was a father, the children are his own. His private life then becomes almost inseparable from his work; although the portraits of the Charpentiers and their friends give a good idea of the circles he frequented, there is an intimacy of quite a different sort in the *Mother and Child* of 1886, which shows Mme Renoir suckling her son Pierre.

Renoir's children appear in his pictures over a long period, each in turn taking over the rôle of model, like the members of a relay team, and keeping alive in their father the spirit of youth. With the passing of the years, however, the theme of childhood lost its hold on the artist, and his sensuous temperament then blossomed out in the pictures devoted almost entirely to the subject of Woman. Nevertheless, in 1918, as if to emphasize, not without a certain nostalgic regret, the distance which now separated him from his earlier work, he painted another *Mother and Child*, identical in composition with the 1886 picture, but very different in style. Both pictures are radiant with the same tender, trusting happiness, despite the thirty years of mingled joys and sorrows which lie between them.

Renoir's little models are well-behaved children, neither forward nor turbulent; on the contrary, they are often rather constrained and

GIRL IN THE GRASS.

serious, and their expressions and smiles are
naturally gentle and grave.   A closer examina-
tion of one of these pictures reveals unsuspected

depths of observation and understanding of the child mind. The female nudes are less rewarding, from this point of view, because there the artist's emotions are not engaged — at least, that is the general belief — but in his portraits Renoir shows very considerable powers of psychological penetration. He can make us look into the future and see how his model's features will have hardened in a few years' time; he captures the precocious vanity of a glance, the coquetry of expectation (pl. 1), or

PIERRE RENOIR. CHILD, 1886

PORTRAIT OF JULIE MANET. STUDY.

the preciosity implicit in the winter costume of
docile, graceful little girls out walking with
their mother (pl. 4). These pictures are
undoubtedly charming, but beneath the grace
of the child, Renoir reveals with implacable
accuracy the woman she will become. His
models put on airs when they pose for him,
and appear at first sight stiff and impersonal, but
he lifts the mask and shows us the real personality behind the pretence.

Renoir was so fond of children that it would be possible to illustrate an account of his life and work by his portraits of children alone. Until 1886, they reflect a period of experiment and apprenticeship, of hesitation and discovery, of great achievement and of even greater promise. His earliest pictures show us the people with whom he is in daily contact; then, when he begins to visit the Charpentiers and their friends, his painting becomes more confident — one might almost say more bourgeois. The prettiness surviving from the days when he had to decorate plates with bouquets of flowers is modified to record the cushioned comfort of middle-class life; the children are dressed in lace and tulle, or wrapped in furs, like precious dolls, well looked-after, lovingly cherished, and protected from the harsher aspects of life. They have nothing to do but to go out for walks — suitably accompanied, of course — and learn to play the piano. Even when he turns from bourgeois subjects to the young acrobats of the Cirque Médrano (1879), Renoir never indulges in picturesque Romantic visions of poverty, all spangles and forced smiles, hiding a melancholy reality; his little girls at the circus are as tranquil, charming, and uncomplicated as those from middle-class homes.

In 1886, with the portrait of Mme Renoir suckling her son Pierre, a change takes place in Renoir's work. The artist is no longer a mere spectator, looking on with affection, but from outside; his own emotions are directly involved in the scene before his eyes. The style, too, is more authoritative ; he has left

HEAD OF A CHILD.

behind the years of study and experiment and freed himself from the influence of Impressionism. The effect of his visit to Italy, however, remains visible in the sharp and accurate drawing which characterises his work for some time (pl. 7) before the full flowering of the healthy sensuality which gives such tremendous warmth and vitality to his later pictures, where red is the dominant colour, as if the artist wants to make us feel the pulsation of the blood beneath the luminous skin. His models no longer belong to any definite social class; they are above all creatures of flesh and blood, living with an intense life which Renoir faithfully records; and the children he paints from now on are his own (pls. 3 and 9).

Thus the discovery of a new source of inspiration in his own family coincided with the attainment of his definitive style, and similarly, when the last of his children, the model for the numerous portraits of Coco, had grown up, the art of Renoir, too, had found its final and permanent form.

It is clear, therefore, that Renoir's portraits of children are by no means a minor feature of his work, for in them he has involuntarily revealed his whole personality as an artist and as a man. The artist generally assumed to be above all the painter of women, the indefatigable admirer of the sensuous charm of the female body, was also a father superlatively sensitive to the touching simplicity of a child's gaze and the ample curves of a baby's mouth—an additional proof, if proof were needed, of the absolute purity of the joy he felt in merely being alive.

LIST OF PLATES

12. GIRLS AT THE PIANO. 1892. *Robert Lehman Collection, New York.*

13. GIRL AGAINST A BLUE BACKGROUND. 1882. *Private collection, Paris.*

14. GIRLS IN A MEADOW. C. 1895. *Sam A. Lewisohn Collection, Metropolitan Museum, New York.*

15. PINK AND BLUE; MESDEMOISELLES CAHEN OF ANTWERP. 1881. *Museo de Arte, Sao Paulo.*

I

4

ACHEVÉ D'IMPRIMER
EN MARS 1969 PAR LES IMPRIMERIES DELMAS
CLICHÉS PERROT ET GRISET